CAMPUS ZOO by

CLARE BARNES, Jr.

DOUBLEDAY & COMPANY, INC.

Garden City, New York 1950

Perhaps those things in the future
Forsan et haec olim
to remember it will please you
meminisse juvabit.

—VIRGIL.

Printed in the United States
First Edition

"Just one more chance . . . please, Dean!"

"Hey, Beamish, lemme borrow your history notes."

"Well, how do you like that? I hope he flunks!"

Tea at the Dean's house.

"I think he's gonna cut the class . . . he's not in sight yet."

Arrival of the package from home.

Upper classmen.

Photo of Dad on the dresser.

Visiting English lecturer caught by school newspaper cameraman.

"Certainly you may have your pin back, Frederic."

"Need I point out, Mr. Bacigaplonski, there are other things beside football?"

Kid with the new convertible.

Pep rally before the Big Game.

"I told 'em just what we'd be wearing. Where do you suppose they are?"

"Figuring how to get in on the party next door."

"The Library . . . day of the Big Game."

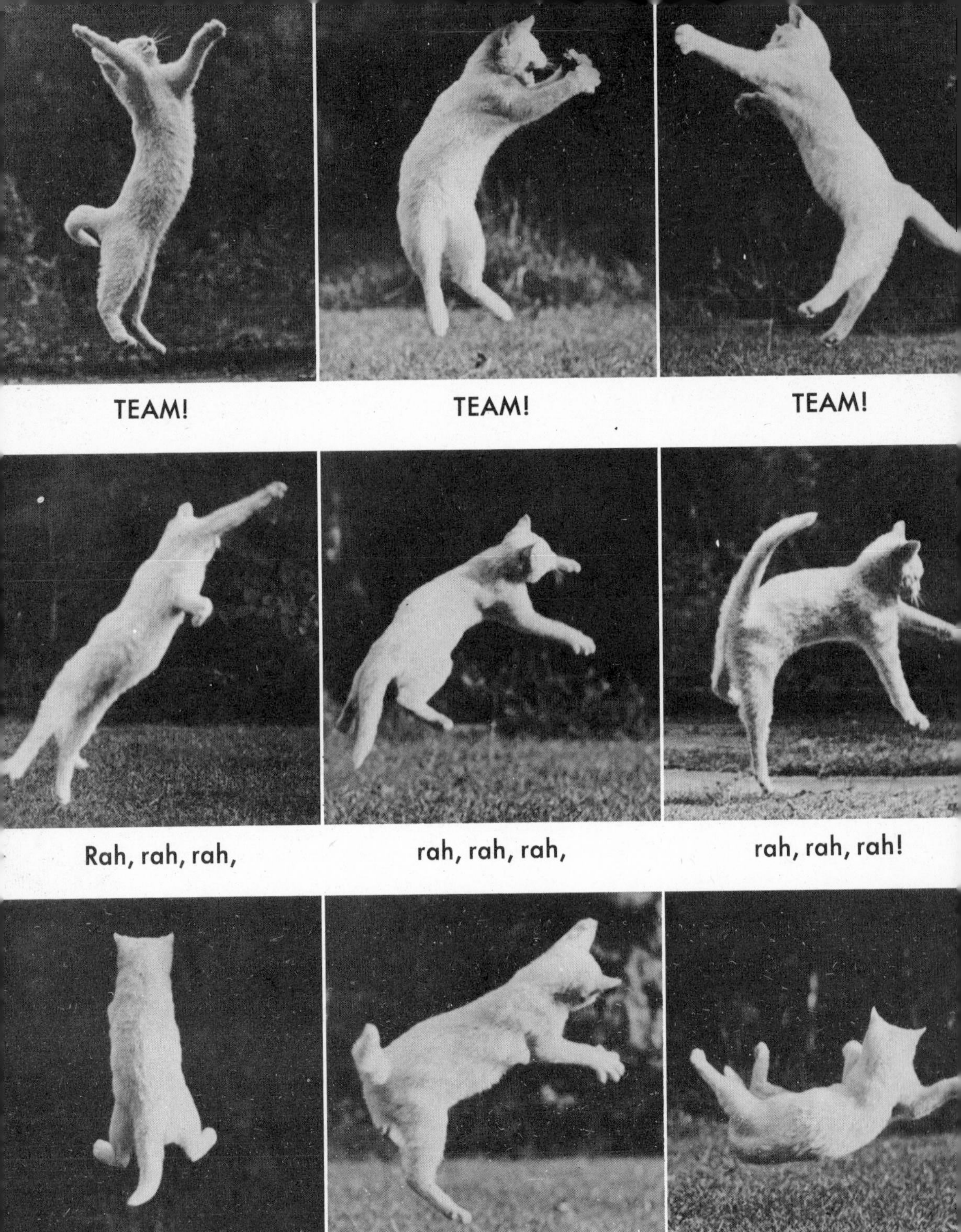

TEAM! TEAM! TEAM!

Rah, rah, rah, rah, rah, rah, rah, rah, rah!

TEAM! TEAM! **TEAM!**

"...down to the thirty, the twenty, the ten...Oooh!
Bacigaplonski's going for a touchdown!"

Opponents lead by twenty points.

Going in for a minute to get his letter.

"I said we'd meet them right here between the halves."

Coach who lost every game.

Campus Shoppe after the fray.

"If *I* have anything to say about it, there'll be a new coach next year."

"Jeez, am I pooped!"

"Why did Ah evuh pick a No'thun school?"

"I'll flunk the whole damn class with this test!"

Dean of Women.

"Prononcez 'eu . . . eu . . . eu'."

"Hmm, not bad, not bad."

And what's so wrong, may I ask, with the Harvard Dental School?

B+ and D−

From the teacher's point of view.

"Are you sure your family's not home?"

"Have you come to the part about married love yet?"

"Whatever can the basketball coach want to see little ol' me for?"

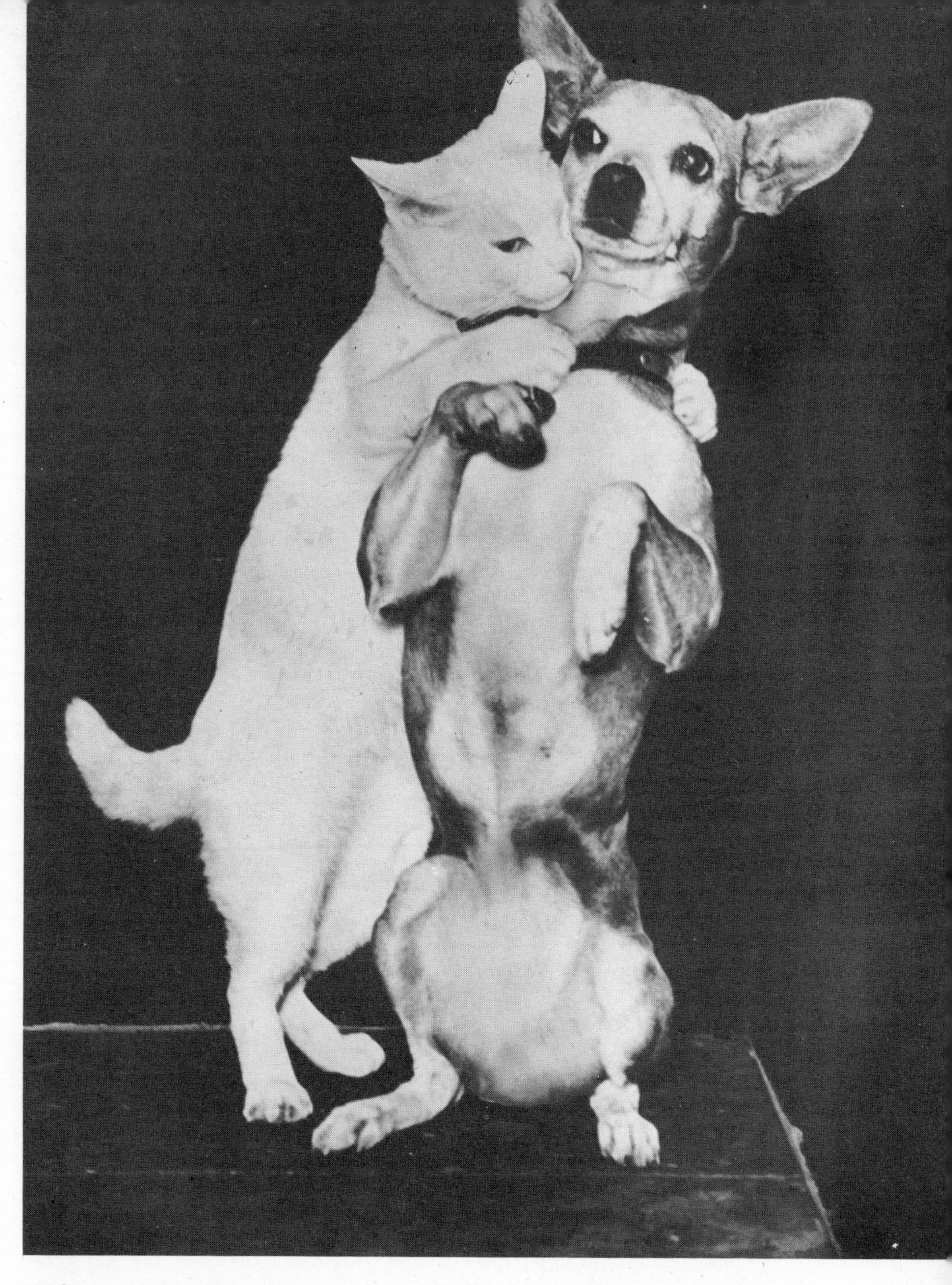

"Those spring house parties must be just loads of fun to go to."

Interesting old photo, possibly by Brady, shows members of the Class of 1864 on Graduation Day.

Statue honoring pioneer leader in higher education for females.

FRATERNITIES

Fraternity legacy whose dad was captain of football.

New pledges.

Initiation night.

The secret grip.

After the initiation.

Girls' Basketball Team.

"Do you think we should add a little more saltpeter?"

Annual Report of the President to the Alumni.

"Tell him I'll be down in a jiffy."

"Skip it . . . here she comes!"

"All right, all right, you don't have to lend me your damned mouton jacket!"

Junior Prom Committee.

"You mean your dance card is filled already?"

Guy who had to take his sister.

Arrival of Prom-trotters.

"May I cut in?"

Gate crashers.

"Dear boy, someday you'll find someone more worthy of your love."

"My, what an interesting hand . . . you should do particularly well in some sort of government work."

"I have a notice here that the Dean wants to see me."

Trying to look inconspicuous during an oral quiz.

Girl who walked home.

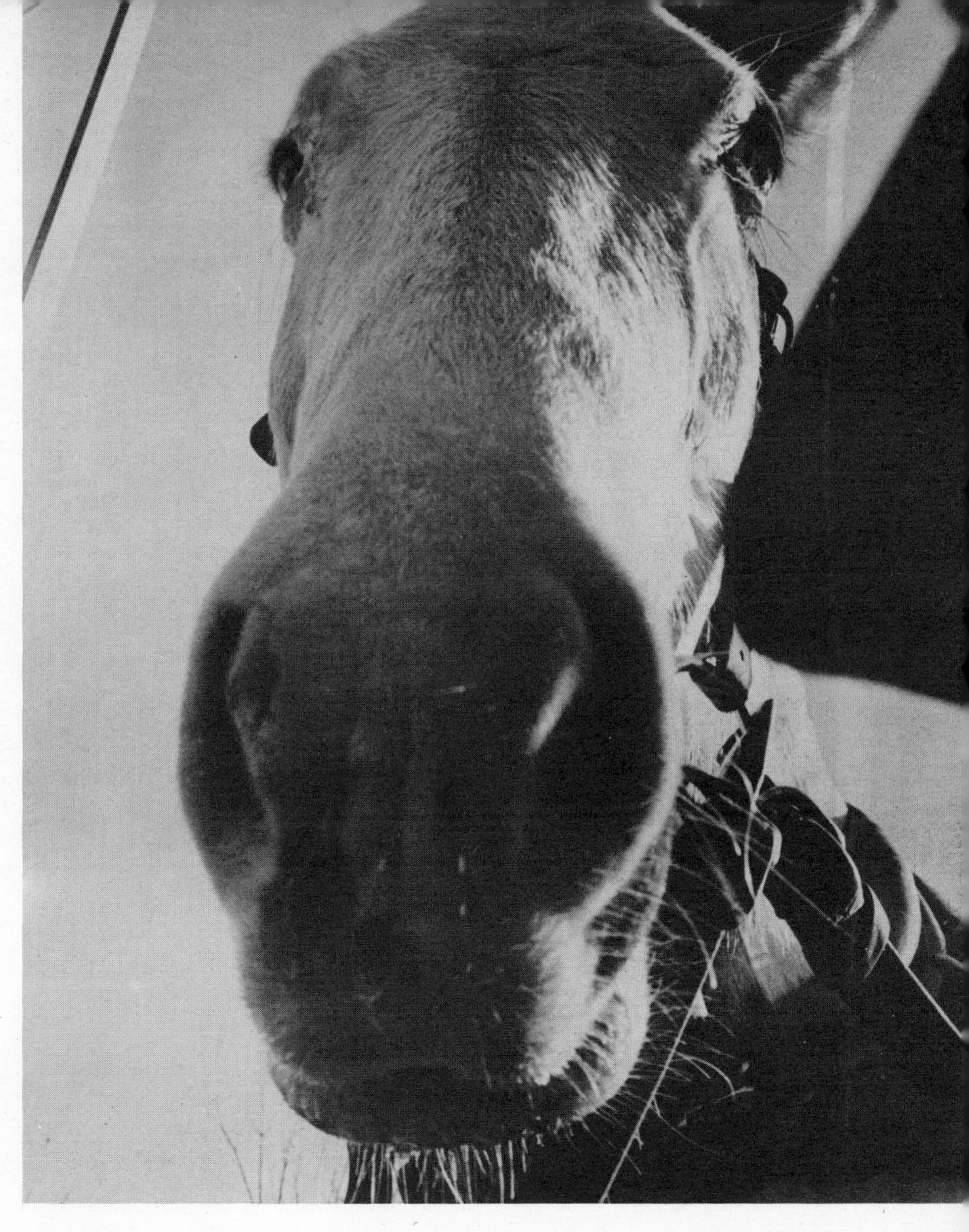

"Is it . . . uh . . . you mean there's somebody else, Lois?"

Town girls.

"I've already given you two months' advance allowance."

The girl who eloped.

Rival sororities.

"Hmm, should I take the exam, or beat it out to the infirmary?"

"Somewhere I've heard that excuse before."

Purely impersonal discussion at the faculty meeting.

Gym class.

Girls' Pajama Party.

"Forty-Beer" Flanagan.

Senior Hoop Race.

Dramat Club rehearsing the witches from *Macbeth*.

REUNION

1947 Triennial.

Class of 1940.

1930.

1920.

1910.

CLASSES

1900.

1890.

1880.

1870.

Townies watching the Alumni Parade.

Elderly prof pretending to remember very well
a former student.

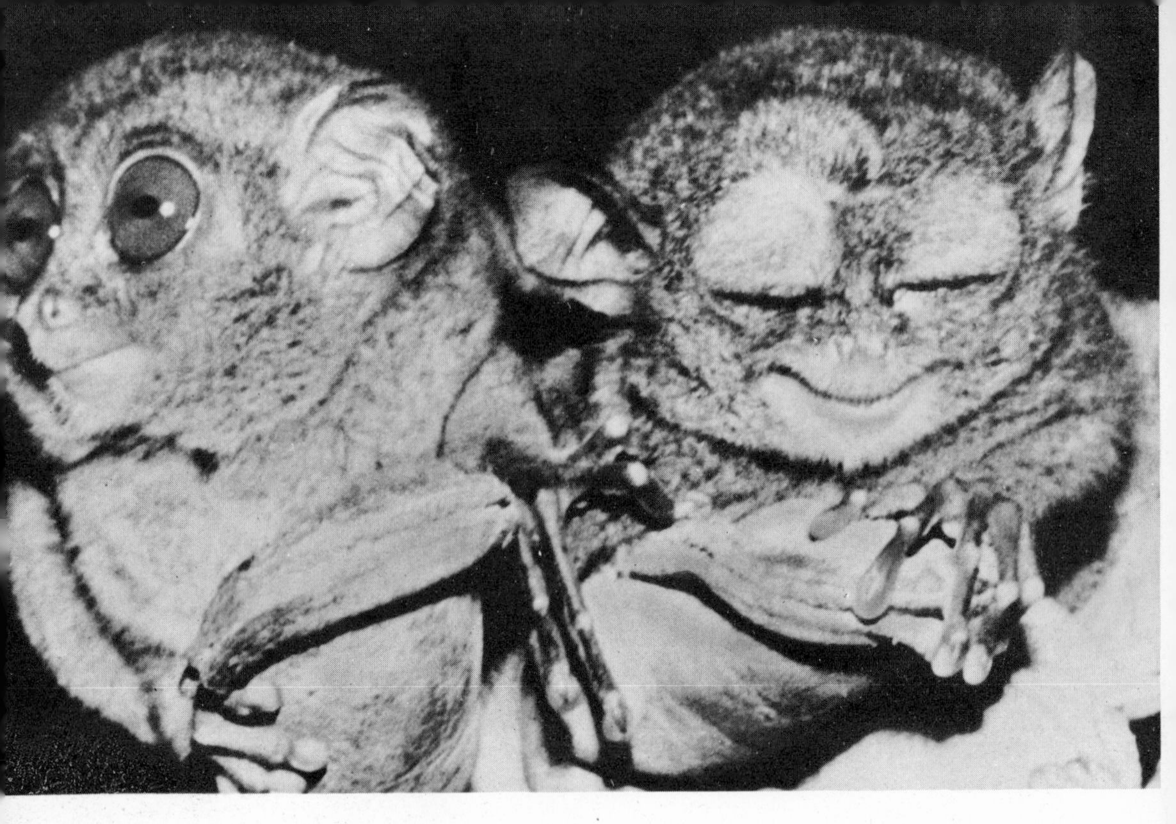

Parents at Commencement.

Graduation Day exercises.

Being presented for an honorary degree.

CLASS VOTES

Wittiest.

Most scholarly.

Best all-round athlete.

Best dressed.

Architect's plan for the University of Tomorrow.

Guy who sat directly ahead of you for four years.

INDEX OF PHOTOGRAPHERS

1. European
2. Green from Lewis
3. International News Photos
4. Rost from Lewis
5. European
6. Wide World
7. European
8. Rost from Lewis
9. Menkin from Lewis
10. European
11. Wide World
12. Lambert from Lewis
13. European
14. Levick from Lewis
15. Wide World
16. European
17. Wide World, European
18. Welgos from Lewis
19. Rittase from Lewis
20. Lambert from Lewis
21. Dorer from Lewis
22. International News Photos
23. International News Photos
24. Wide World
25. Lambert from Lewis
26. European
27. Morris from Lewis
28. European
30. Wide World
31. International News Photos
32. Wide World
33. Lambert from Lewis
34. Frederic Lewis
35. International News Photos
36. European
37. Field Museum from Wide World
38. European
39. European and Frederic Lewis
40. Wide World
41. Wide World
42. Wide World
43. European
44. Wide World
45. Stevens from Lewis
46. European and Frederic Lewis
47. European and Wide World
48. Wide World
49. Wide World
50. European
52. Woolf from Lewis
53. Wide World
54. Woolf from Lewis
55. International News Photo
56. European
57. Schmidt from Lewis
58. Krainin from Lewis
59. Arnfeld from European
60. Hirz from Lewis
62. Welgos from Lewis
64. Wide World
65. H. M. H. Kimball

66, 67. Lewis, Keystone, Wide World

68. Watson from European
69. Wide World
70. International News Photos
71. Wide World
72. European
73. (b) International; (d) Lewis
74. International News Photos
75. Hamar from Lewis